599.79
PAP

124453

Capital City Academy
Learning Centre
Doyle Gardens
London NW10 3ST

Tel: 0208 8388778

0 4 OCT 2005

CAPITAL CITY ACADEMY
LEARNING CENTRE
DOYLE GARDENS NW10
0208838877

WILDLIFE AT RISK

SEALS AND SEA LIONS

Vassili Papastavrou

WILDLIFE AT RISK

Bears
Birds of Prey
Elephants
Gorillas
Monkeys
Pandas
Rhinos
Seals and Sea Lions
Tigers
Whales and Dolphins

599.79 PAP

Book editor: Liz Miller
Series designer: Marilyn Clay

Cover: A Moulting grey seal pup.

First published in 1991 by
Wayland (Publishers) Ltd
61 Western Road, Hove
East Sussex, BN3 1JD, England

© Copyright 1991 Wayland (Publishers) Ltd

British Library Cataloguing in Publication Data
Papastavrou, Vassili
  Seals
  1. Mammals : Seals
  I. Title   II. Series
  599.745

ISBN 0-7502-0146-0

Typeset by Dorchester Typesetting Group Ltd
Printed and bound in Italy by L.E.G.O. S.p.A.

Contents

Introducing pinnipeds 4

Types of pinniped 8

Life in the sea 12

At risk from hunters 18

Pinnipeds in danger 21

The future for pinnipeds 28

Glossary 30

Further reading 31

Useful addresses 31

Index 32

Words printed in **bold** are explained in the glossary on page 30.

INTRODUCING PINNIPEDS

Seals, sea lions and walruses all belong to the group of **mammals** known as pinnipeds. The word pinniped means 'fin-footed'. The flippers are shaped like paddles to help the animal swim through the water. Just like other mammals, pinnipeds give birth to live young which are fed on milk. All mammals are warm-blooded and need to breathe air to stay alive. Mammals that live in the sea are called marine mammals. Pinnipeds are one example of a group of marine mammals. Whales and dolphins are another group. However, unlike whales and dolphins, pinnipeds need to come to shore to **mate** and to give birth: this is called hauling-out.

A Weddell seal pops its head through a breathing hole in the ice.

Galapagos sea lions – all sea lions have two back flippers.

Below *The New Zealand fur seal is found south of Australia, and on various islands south of New Zealand.*

Thirty million years ago, the early **ancestors** of pinnipeds lived on land and looked like bears. Over time they changed to become better suited to life in the sea. They became more **streamlined** so that they could move easily through the water. In this way they were able to catch fish and find new sources of food. The fastest pinniped can swim at 25 kph. On land, movement is more difficult. However, sea lions are able to turn their back flippers under themselves and can move easily on land.

Grey seal pups have thick white fur which becomes grey as they get older.

Pinnipeds are well equipped for life in the sea. Seals and sea lions have large eyes which help them hunt their food underwater. They have a thick layer of fat, called blubber, which helps them to keep warm. Some also have thick fur. Staying warm is especially important for the animals that swim in the ice-cold waters of the **Arctic** and **Antarctic**.

When seals are on land, they can get too hot. They cool themselves by flipping sand onto their back, waving their flippers in the air, or by dipping them in pools of water.

Southern elephant seals flip sand onto their backs to protect them from the heat of the sun.

The New Zealand fur seal is an eared seal, as you can see.

There are 34 **species** (or kinds) of pinniped and these are split up into three families – eared seals, earless seals and walruses. The eared seals have **lobes** to their ears, like humans. The earless seals just have a tiny hole. The third family is the walrus. Walruses have long teeth, called tusks, which they use to help them climb out of the water and on to the ice. The walrus is the only member of its family.

Pinnipeds are a fascinating group of animals. Some pinnipeds can dive deeper than one kilometre below the surface of the sea. Others can move faster on land than a human. When caring for their **pups**, some pinnipeds do not eat any food for over a month.

Over the past two hundred years pinnipeds have been killed in very large numbers by humans. Now they are in danger from other threats such as **pollution**.

TYPES OF PINNIPED

Walrus

Walruses live in shallow areas of the cold Arctic. There are two **populations** of walrus. One population is in the North Pacific and the other is in the North Atlantic. Both the males and the females have long tusks which have many uses. The tusks help the walrus to move about and to defend itself against attacks by polar bears.

Walruses like to stay close to the edge of the ice. As the ice melts in the summer, the walruses move north. In the winter, they move south again.

Male walruses haul-out in large groups.

Crabeater seal

This crabeater seal lives on pack-ice in the Antarctic.

Crabeater seals live in the Antarctic. Here there are about 30 million of these animals. There are more crabeater seals than any other pinniped. Males and females are about the same size and each weighs over 200 kg. Crabeater seals have long snouts and are quite slim. The young seals are silvery coloured, with brown markings on their sides. Over the year the coat fades until it is almost white.

Crabeaters usually live on the drifting **pack-ice** but sometimes move far inland. One crabeater was found on a **glacier** over 100 km from open water.

Californian sea lion

Californian sea lions can be seen in most zoos. They are very intelligent animals and it is easy to teach them tricks. One trick many **captive** sea lions are taught is to balance a ball on the end of the nose.

The males are about 2.4 m long and weigh up to 300 kg.

A performing sea lion in Miami's seaquarium, in the USA.

Females are smaller and weigh about 100 kg. These sea lions usually eat squid and octopus. Sometimes they also eat fish.

Most Californian sea lions live along the coast of California. About 30,000 animals live on the Galapagos Islands, which are west of South America. There also used to be a population of these seals living in Japan, but we do not know whether there are any left.

Wild Californian sea lions are often curious and will approach swimmers.

Grey seal

There are only two species of seal that live in British waters, the grey seal and the common seal. Around Britain there are at least 25,000 common seals and about 100,000 grey seals. This is almost half of the world's grey seals.

In 1914 there were perhaps as few as 500 grey seals to be found around Britain.

Common seals are graceful swimmers and divers.

Although this female grey seal looks fat, she can escape quickly into the water if she needs to.

Since then, their numbers have been increasing. This is partly because there are now **restrictions** on hunting grey seals. Also, people no longer live on some of Britain's most distant islands. Now that they are not disturbed in these places, grey seals are able to **breed** in peace.

LIFE IN THE SEA

Pinnipeds make use of a great variety of **habitats**. Animals such as the Guadalupe fur seal and the Mediterranean monk seal usually haul-out in caves. Others haul-out on ice or rocks. Many more pinnipeds live in the cold waters of the Arctic and the Antarctic than in the **tropics**. Perhaps there is more food for them in these cold habitats. In the tropics, food is hard to find.

There is little space for these walruses to haul-out along this rocky shore.

The time depth recorder attached to the back of this Antarctic fur seal will record information on each dive.

It is very difficult to watch pinnipeds at sea and for this reason we know very little about what they do away from land. Recently, scientists have attached time-depth recorders (TDRs) to seals. A TDR is able to record the depth of every single dive which the animal makes. Using TDRs, we know that Weddell seals can dive 600 m below the surface: they can stay underwater for over one hour.

However, southern elephant seals can dive even deeper. The greatest depth recorded so far is 1,500 m. What is even more amazing is that they spend very little time at the surface. An elephant seal usually spends less than three minutes at the surface in between dives. At night, the dives are shallower, because the fish and squid which the seals eat move closer to the surface in the dark.

This Weddell seal takes her pup diving. They stay underwater for a longer period each time, until the pup can dive alone.

Fish or squid are the most common food for pinnipeds. The grey seal eats a variety of fish, including sand eels and salmon. Different animals form part of the diet of other seals. Walruses swim upside-down and search along the sea-bed for clams. A walrus can eat up to six clams in a minute. Crabeater seals take mouthfuls of sea water and strain out krill through their specially adapted teeth. Krill are tiny shrimp-like animals. They are an important source of food for many animals in the Antarctic, including whales and Antarctic fur seals. Krill are also caught by fishermen.

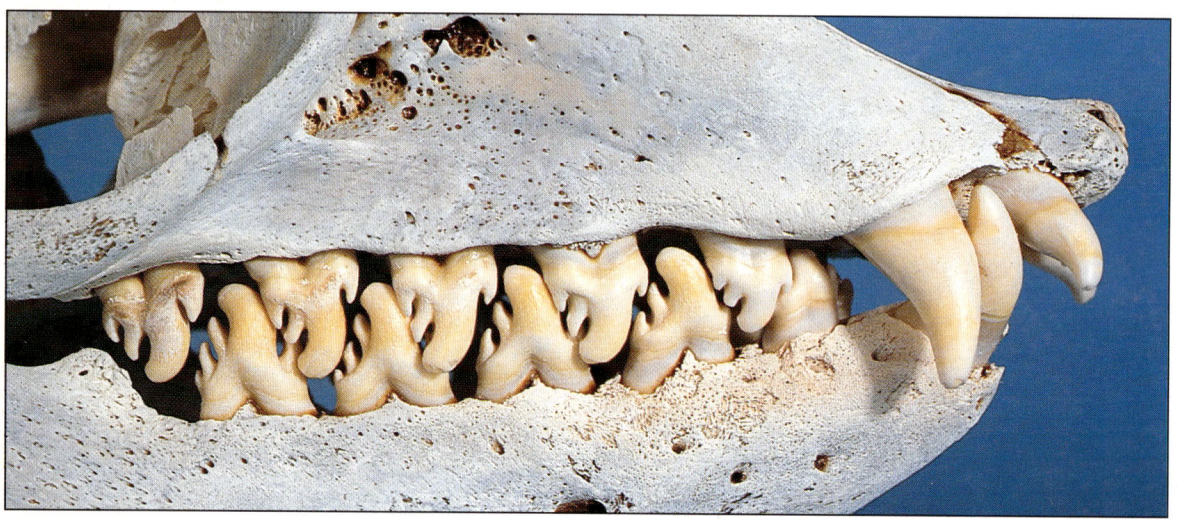

The skull of this crabeater seal shows how its teeth can sieve tiny krill.

Left *A single krill. Krill are very small – the biggest are only 3 cm long.*

Some species of seal eat other seals. Leopard seals are fierce hunters and eat crabeater seals, fur seals and elephant seals. Almost all crabeater seals have wounds made by leopard seals. Leopard seals will also attack and eat penguins.

Adelie penguins are sometimes attacked by a leopard seal, waiting in the waters below.

A swimming leopard seal may break through the ice above to attack its prey.

Sometimes, penguins can be seen crowded around the water's edge. None of the penguins wants to be the first to jump, in case there is a hungry leopard seal waiting. Leopard seals are usually shy of humans. However, there are some frightening stories of them attacking divers.

The huge male southern elephant seal is much bigger than the female.

The pinnipeds that breed on dry land usually haul-out in large groups. This is because there are only a few places that are suitable. The male of most of these species is very much larger than the female. For example, an adult male southern elephant seal may weigh nearly four tonnes. The females are much smaller and weigh less than one tonne.

Males try to mate with as many females as possible. There is a big advantage for a male in being larger than any other male. Males arrive first at the breeding beaches and fight to see who is the strongest. The largest males have control over the most females. Sometimes one elephant seal will mate with more than 100 females.

Male southern elephant seals become injured when they fight over females.

Like all baby mammals, Australian sea lion pups suck milk from their mothers.

The pinnipeds that breed on ice are very different and some species haul-out far away from each other. Others, such as the harp seal, live together in their thousands. Males and females are usually the same size. Males do not fight each other over females.

Most pinnipeds give birth soon after they haul-out. Pinniped milk is rich in fat and allows the pup to grow fast. During the time that the pup is feeding, the mother does not eat much and becomes very thin. Earless seals rarely eat while they are feeding the pup with their milk.

AT RISK FROM HUNTERS

Pinnipeds are hunted by other animals. In some areas, they are a major source of food for great white sharks. Common seals, Californian sea lions, elephant seals and southern fur seals are all attacked by sharks. Those that survive have huge scars.

Many species of pinnipeds fall victim to orcas (killer whales). The remains of fourteen seals were found inside the stomach of one orca. Orcas often hunt together. They have been seen herding groups of sea lions into a tight bunch. The orcas will then take it in turns to feed on the terrified sea lions. Off the coast of Patagonia in South America, orcas even take seal pups from the surf.

Along the Valdez Peninsula, off the coast of Argentina, orcas almost come out of the water to catch sea lions.

Above *This Soviet hunter has caught a Baikal seal in a net.*

Today, some pinnipeds are still hunted. The South American fur seal is killed for its oil and fur. In Alaska, many thousands of walruses are being slaughtered just for their tusks. Now that it is against the law to sell elephant tusks, hunters are killing walruses instead. Only the tusks are taken and the rest is wasted. The walruses' ivory tusks are made into ornaments and jewellery and sold around the world.

Below *These expensive fur coats are made from seal skins.*

In the past, many species of pinnipeds were hunted by people. When they were killed, the blubber was boiled to make oil and their skins were sold. The story is the same as the story of whaling: the sealers took so many animals that there were almost none left. Now, pinnipeds are at risk from other threats too.

So many northern elephant seals were hunted for their oil that they almost became **extinct**. By 1890 there were only about 20 animals left. Now, they are no longer hunted and numbers have increased to over 100,000. All these came from the original 20 animals. Because they are so closely related they are all very similar. In any species, it is important that animals are different from each other so that the species can survive changes to its habitat. We do not know whether these elephant seals will be able to cope with any such changes.

An elephant seal's 'trunk' gets bigger when the animal is angry.

PINNIPEDS IN DANGER

Fur seals often become tangled in plastic **packing straps** that have been thrown away. As the seal grows, the strap becomes tighter. It cuts into the flesh and slowly strangles the animal. Both northern and Antarctic fur seals are at risk from this

The wound on the neck of this young Antarctic fur seal is caused by thrown-away plastic.

lingering death. This may be one reason why there are now fewer fur seals living on the Pribilof Islands (between the USSR and Alaska).

Many pinnipeds become tangled in fishing nets and drown. South African fur seals are caught and drown in trawl nets. A new type of fishing called drift netting is a major threat to pinnipeds and other marine animals. Drift nets may be 70 km long and are almost invisible in the water.

In many parts of the world, fishermen blame seals for the lack of fish in the sea for them to catch. The fishermen then say that some seals must be killed. The real reason for the lack of fish is overfishing by humans. Seals often take different kinds of fish that the fishermen do not want to catch. Because seals were wrongly blamed, many harp seals used to be hunted in the Barents Sea, and off Canada and Norway.

It is impossible for this Antarctic fur seal to escape from the net.

Steller's sea lions live in a number of places in the North Pacific, including the Aleutian Islands. Their numbers have been falling for 30 years. In 1957 there were about 140,000, but now there are perhaps as few as 25,000 Steller's sea lions left. One possible reason is that they may be suffering from a disease. The disease could be stopping the sea lions from breeding successfully.

We do not understand why the number of Steller's sea lions has fallen, but something must be done to save them.

Perhaps they become tangled in fishing nets or are shot by fishermen. Another idea is that fishermen are taking too many of the fish which the sea lions need to eat. If we are to save these animals, we need to stop boats fishing close to where they live.

For many years people have used the seas for dumping poisonous chemicals such as PCBs. PCBs are chemicals used in the manufacture of plastics and electrical equipment. **Pesticides** such as DDT wash into rivers and then find their way into the sea. Now we have found out that these chemicals build up in the bodies of pinnipeds.

Many poisonous chemicals are released into the sea from pipelines such as this.

All over the world, people are polluting the rivers which flow into the sea.

Pollutants can even be passed on from a mother to her pup in the milk.

In the Baltic Sea over three-quarters of the grey seals are unable to breed. Scientists have discovered that the seals are suffering from the effects of high levels of pollution.

The Baikal seal is only found in Lake Baikal (in the USSR). Lake Baikal is the largest freshwater lake in the world. These seals are threatened by pollution from many factories along the shores of the lake. Many Russians are fighting to save this important lake and the animals that live in it.

Below *The Baikal seal is the only freshwater seal. It is at risk from pollution.*

Paper mills pour their waste into Lake Baikal.

The Mediterranean monk seal is the only pinniped in real danger of becoming extinct. Perhaps only 500 of these animals are left. Monk seals are often disturbed by humans and now come ashore only on quiet islands, deserted beaches or caves. In the last century, monk seals were hunted in large numbers for their skins. Now, they face other threats. Fishermen think they are eating too much fish and shoot them. Some seals get tangled up in fishing nets and drown. Many tourists go to the Mediterranean for their holidays and there are almost no beaches left for these seals to live in peace. If we are to save these animals, we need to know more about them. We must also set up nature reserves where they can be left alone.

The shy Mediterranean monk seal is now extremely rare.

Some seals, like this northern elephant seal, have to live among the rubbish people throw away.

In 1988, common seals around the coasts of Britain and Northern Europe became ill and started dying in large numbers. Around 3,000 animals died in Britain and perhaps up to 14,000 in the rest of Europe. Scientists soon realized that the seals were dying from a newly discovered disease.

The disease may have been carried to Europe by Arctic seals travelling further south than usual. Pollution in the North Sea may have made the animals weaker and more likely to die from the disease. The surviving common seals may now be affected less by the disease. We hope their numbers may soon increase.

THE FUTURE FOR PINNIPEDS

Although pinnipeds are at risk, there has been much success in the fight to save them.

Many people in Europe have **campaigned** against the killing of baby seals. These baby seals are called 'white-coats'. Now the **EEC** has made new laws which prevent anyone importing the skins of white-coats. If the hunters cannot make money selling the skins, they will not hunt them any more. Then these beautiful animals will be left to live undisturbed.

A Greenpeace campaigner sprays a pup with dye so that its coat is worthless to hunters.

Tourists, visiting northern Canada, meet a baby harp seal on the ice.

In Canada, the International Fund for Animal Welfare (IFAW) has worked for many years to stop the hunting of seals. Now IFAW takes tourists by helicopter on to the ice to see baby seals for themselves. The money that the tourists pay will replace money earned by selling seal skins.

In South Africa, there was a plan to kill many fur seals and sell the skins. The meat was going to be made into pet food. However, people around the world **protested** and the hunt was called off.

All around the world, there are scientists studying pinnipeds. Some of the research shows that seals do not usually steal fish from fishermen. Further research is needed to find out about the other threats which they face. Many people care about this beautiful group of animals. With your help, we can make sure that seals, sea lions and walruses can live in peace.

Let's hope that in future we will only see fur coats on live animals, such as this harp seal pup.

Glossary

Ancestors Animals in the past from which present-day animals come.

Antarctic The most southerly parts of the world: the Antarctic is very cold.

Arctic The most northerly parts of the world: the Arctic is very cold.

Breed To produce babies.

Campaigned Asked for support from others for a good cause.

Captive Kept in human care. For example, keeping a seal in a pool.

EEC A group of European countries that share farming, trade and food production laws.

Extinct When the last animal belonging to a particular species has died.

Glacier A frozen river. Icebergs break off from the ends of glaciers.

Habitat The natural home of a plant or animal.

Lobes The fleshy, outer parts of ears, made of skin and fat.

Mammals Animals which are warm-blooded and have hair or fur. Mammals give birth to live young which they feed with their own milk.

Mate To come together as a male and a female to produce babies.

Pack-ice Ice which forms in the sea in very cold places.

Packing straps Thrown away strips of plastic which were once used for tying up boxes and crates.

Pesticides Poisonous chemicals which are used to kill insects or other pests.

Pollutants Poisonous chemicals released into the environment by humans.

Pollution The harm caused to the natural environment when humans release dangerous substances into it.

Populations A group of animals all of the same species which live in the same place and breed together.

Protested Showing disagreement for something.

Pups The name for young seals.

Restrictions Laws which limit, for example, the number of seals that can be hunted.

Species A group of animals that is different from all other groups. Only members of the same species can breed together.

Streamlined Having a smooth flowing shape that passes easily through air or water.

Tropics The parts of the world which are very hot, which lie in a band each side of the equator.

Further reading

The Common Seal Paul Thomson (Shire Natural History, 1989).
The Grey Seal Sheila Anderson (Shire Natural History, 1988).
Seals Lucy Baker (Two-Can, 1990).
Seals Michael Bright (Franklin Watts, 1990)

Seals and Sea Lions John Cloudsley-Thompson (Wayland, 1981).
Seasons of the Seal Fred Bruemmer and Brian Davies (Lorraine Grey Publications, 1988).

Useful addresses

If you would like to get involved in wildlife conservation you might like to join one of the organizations listed below.

Greenpeace
30-31 Islington Green
London N1 8XE

Greenpeace has offices in most major countries.

International Fund for Animal Welfare (IFAW)
PO Box 193
Yarmouth Port
MA 02675 USA

Royal Society for the Prevention of Cruelty to Animals (RSPCA)
Causeway
Horsham
West Sussex RH12 1HG

Picture acknowledgements
Biofotos 24 (left); Bruce Coleman Ltd/Francisco Erize 15 (right); Greenpeace 19 (below), 24 (left), 28 (above). All other photographs were supplied by Oxford Scientific Films by: Tony Martin *cover*, Doug Allen 4, 9, 13, 15 (left), 19 (above), 25 (both); Tom Arnbom 27, 28; Joe Dorsey 10 (left); Jeff Foott 18; G J Gilbert 14 (both); Dr G S Grant 26; Susan Jones 10 (right); Lon Lauber 8, 12 (right); T S McCann 16 (both); Ben Osborne 6 (below), 12 (left), 21, 22; Richard Packwood 17; Hans Reinhard 28 (below); Carl Roessler 5 (above); Paul Thompson 11 (both), 20; Kim Westerskov 5 (below); Graham Wren 6 (above).

Index

Alaska   19, 21
Antarctic   6, 12, 14
Arctic   6, 12, 27
Atlantic   8
Australia   5, 17

Baikal seal   19, 25
Baltic Sea   24
Blubber   6, 19
Breeding   11, 16, 17, 22, 24
Britain   11, 27

Campaigns   28, 29
Canada   22, 28
Common seal   18, 27
Crabeater seal   9, 14, 15

Disease   23, 27
Diving   7, 12, 13, 15

Eared seals   7, 17
Earless seals   7, 17
EEC   28
Elephant seals   13, 15, 16, 18, 20
Europe   27, 28

Fighting   16, 17
Fishing   22, 23, 26, 29
Flippers   4, 6
Food   5, 6, 12, 13, 14, 23

Fur seals   21
 Antarctic   12, 14, 21
 Guadelupe   12
 New Zealand   5, 7
 Northern   21
 South African   21, 29
 South American   19
 Southern   18

Galapagos   10
Grey seal   11, 14

Habitats   12, 20
Harp seal   17, 22, 28, 29
Hauling-out   4, 12, 16, 17
Hunting   11, 18, 19, 20, 23, 28, 29

Japan   10

Killer whales   18
Krill   14

Leopard seal   15

Mediterranean monk seal   12, 16

New Zealand   5, 7
North Sea   27
Norway   22

Orcas   18

Pacific   8, 23
Penguins   15
Pollution   24, 25, 27
Protests   28, 29
Pups   7, 17, 18, 24

Sea lions   4, 6, 10, 18, 23, 29
 Australian   17
 Californian   10, 18
 Galapagos   5
 Steller's   23
Sharks   18, 20
Skins/fur   19, 26, 28

Teeth   14
Threats   7, 29
Time depth recorders (TDR)   12
Tourists   26, 28, 29
Tropics, the   12
Tusks   7, 8, 19

USA   10, 18
USSR   19, 21, 25

Walruses   4, 7, 8, 14, 19, 29
Weddell seal   4, 12, 13
Whales   14, 19
White-coats   28

CAPITAL CITY ACADEMY
LEARNING CENTRE
DOYLE GARDENS NW10
0208838877